NEW English Adventure

Student's Book with Workbook

LEVEL 4

Tessa Lochowski
Anne Worrall
with José Luis Morales

Pearson

Pearson Education Limited
Edinburgh Gate
Harlow
Essex CM20 2JE
England
and Associated Companies throughout the world.

www.pearsonELT.com

© Pearson Education Limited 2015. This edition of New English Adventure Level 4 is published by Pearson Education do Brasil, 2016, by arrangement of Pearson Education Limited.

Copyright © 2016 Disney Enterprises, Inc. All rights reserved. Pixar characters and artwork Copyright © Disney and Pixar.

Materials and characters from the movie *Cars*. Copyright ©2016 Disney/Pixar.
Disney/Pixar elements © Disney/Pixar, not including underlying vehicles owned by third parties, and, if applicable: Cadillac Coupe DeVille, Chevrolet and H-1 hummer are trademarks of General Motors; Dodge, Hudson Hornet, Plymouth Superbird are trademarks of Chrysler LLC; Jeep® and the Jeep® grille design are registered trademarks of Chrysler Llc; Fairlane is a trademark of Ford Motor Company; FIAT is a trademark of FIAT S.p.A.; Mack is a registered trademark of Mack Trucks, Inc.; Mercury and Model T are registered trademarks of Ford Motor Company; Pontiac GTO is a trademark of General Motors; Porsche is a trademark of Porsche; Sarge's rank insignia design used with the approval of the U.S. Army; Volkswagen trademarks, design patents and copyrights are used with the approval of the owner Volkswagen AG; Background inspired by the Cadillac Ranch by Ant Farm (Lord, Michels and Marquez) © 1974

The rights of Tessa Lochowski and Anne Worrall to be identified as authors of this work have been asserted by them in accordance with the Copyright, Designs and Patents Act 1988.

Additional material provided by Jose Luis Morales.

All rights reserved; no part of this publication may be reproduced, stored in a retrieval system, or transmitted in any form or by any means, electronic, mechanical, photocopying, recording, or otherwise without the prior written permission of the Publishers.

First published 2016

New English Adventure Level 4 Student's book
ISBN 978-1-292-14131-2

Set in Frutiger Lt Pro (75 Black, 55 Roman)

Printed in Brazil by Reproset RPPA 224207

Head of Product- Pearson Brazil: Gabriela Diuana

Product Manager- Pearson Brazil: Marjorie Robles

Product Coordinator and Editor: Priscila Marconi

Editor: Rhiannon Ball

Art and Design: Alto Contraste SP

Audio: Maximal Studio

Pearson Education do Brasil would like to thank Gisele Aga for her feedback during the development.

Illustrated by Comicup, David Belmonte, John Lund, Gustavo Mazali, Davide Ortu, Roger Stewart.

Special thanks to Basia Jagiełło, Adam Kielak, Mikołaj Kielak and Hania Medyńska for their drawings.

We are grateful to the following for permission to reproduce copyright material:

Page 50: Figures from http://scouts.org.uk/home/.Text adapted from http://scouts.org.uk/home/, with permission from the Scout Association

In some instances we have been unable to trace the owners of copyright material, and we would appreciate any information that would enable us to do so.

The publisher would like to thank the following for their kind permission to reproduce their photographs:

(Key: b-bottom; c-centre; l-left; r-right; t-top)

123RF.com: 42cl, Ruth Black 18/4, Cliffdabbs 34tl, Jaren Wicklund 50tc, Luis Louro 60cl, racorn 29/3, Raptorcaptor 58/4, Shane Trotter 4 (worried), Zechal 57cr; **The Scout Association 2007:** 50br; **Alamy Images:** Allstar Picture Library 26/2, Jack Sullivan 26tr, ZUMAPRESS.com / NewSport / Craig Brough 26/3; **Corbis:** Tim Clayton 26/4; **Fotolia.com:** Aleksandr 65/2, Alekss 53 (grass), Altanaka 50bl, Anakondasp 65cr, Anrymos 5tl, AntonioDiaz 61tc, ARochau 10bc, Asierromero 10tr, Andrew Barker 58/1, Mariusz Blach 18/1, BlueOrange Studio 17cl, 60c, Bourbon Numérik 57tl, Chris Brignell 65 (hat), Oscar Brunet 45cl, By-studio 12 (snowing), Sergiy Bykhunenko 4 (sad), 14c/1, Rob Byron 20cr, Cheryl Casey 10br, Jacek Chabraszewski 60cr, Chomnancoffee 61tr, Dekanaryas 4cl, EcoView 52l, 53/4, Eisenhans 28l, ElinaManninen 65 (surfboard), Elnur 65 (shorts), C Farmer 61c, Fasphotographic 5bl, Francescodemarco 58/2, Furmananna 18/2, Vladislav Gajic 61tl, Gelpi 3bl, 3br, 4l, 5br, 49cl, 49cr, 65/3, 65/4, Goodluz50d 50tl, Hetizia 20l, Highwaystarz 61cr, JackF 29/4, JJAVA 66c, Johnny-ka 12cl, Kadmy 45cr, Alexandra Karamyshev 65 (swimsuit), Serhiy Kobyakov 4cr, 10tc, Dusan Kostic 61cl, leiana 42c, Liandstudio 45c, Gino Santa Maria 20 (jumping), Mariemilyphotos 52r, Maska82 5bc, Maxximmm 10tl, Monkey Business 18/3, Nanettegrebe 14c/3, Andrei Nekrassov 34br, Sergey Nivens 45tl, Emin Ozkan 12cr, Pab_map 28 (cafe), Jacques Palut 52cr, Phanuwatnandee 14t/2, Phillip du Plessis 53/3, Rabbit75_fot 34tr, Sergey Ryzhov 50bc, Irina Schmidt 17cr, SergiyN 14c/4, T Sirikorn 14c/2, Sixdays 5tr, Sjhuls 20r, Suksao 58/3, Svetamart 5tc, 21tc, Turi 28r, Uwe Bumann 57tr, Valiza14 21tl, Vichie81 14t/4, WavebreakMediaMicro 4r, 45tc, 65/1, Piotr Wawrzyniuk 28cl, Wckiw 20 (talking), Wolfelarry 65cl, Yurolaitsalbert 10cr; **Getty Images:** Ian Walton 26/1; **Imagestate Media:** John Foxx Collection 52cl, 66tl; **iStock:** 68tr, 69tr; **MIXA Co., Ltd:** 42cr; **Pearson Education Ltd:** Studio 8 20cl, 21cl, Jon Barlow 3tl, Gareth Boden 37, 54, Trevor Clifford 3tr, Naki Kouyioumtzis 34bl, Rafal Trubisz 9bl, 9br, 17b, 25bl, 25br, 30, 33, 41, 49bl, 49br, 57bl, 57br, 65b; **Shutterstock.com:** AVAVA 21cr, CandyBox Images 45tr, Rich Carey 66br, Creative Travel Projects 17tl, Det-anan 14t/1, Dutourdumonde 12r, Fotohunter 53 (seeds), Lim Yong Hian 28cr, Hxdbzxy 29/2, Peter Kirillov 66bl, D. Kucharski K. Kucharska 53/2, Ru Bai Le 29/1, Ilaszlo 52 (leaves), Aleksandr Markin 60l, Mikhail Melnikov 53cl, michaeljung 66tr, Monkey Business Images 10bl, Sari Oneal 12 (cold), Thomas M Perkins 53cr, Sergey Peterman 21c, PhotoSky 66cr, QQ7 34cl, RM 53/1, Sailorr 42tl, Snehit 14t/3, Audrey Snider-Bell 52 (crocodile), Jordan Tan 57tc, Suzanne Tucke 21tr, AH Turner 60r, Vaclav Volrab 17tr, Tom Wang 12l, WDG Photo 28 (park); **Sozaijiten:** 42tr

All other images © Pearson Education

Every effort has been made to trace the copyright holders and we apologise in advance for any unintentional omissions. We would be pleased to insert the appropriate acknowledgement in any subsequent edition of this publication.

NEW English Adventure

Student's Book

LEVEL 4

Contents	page
Hello	2
1. I'm happy	4
2. It's snowing	12
3. I'm dancing	20
4. There's a park	28
5. My day	36
6. My hobbies	44
7. Lions eat meat	52
8. I like surfing	60

Contents	page
Harvest Festival	68
Bonfire Night	69
New Year's Eve	70
Valentine's Day	71
Mother's Day	72
Cut-outs	73
Workbook	89
Picture Dictionary	161
Stickers	163

Go to https://newenglishadventure.pearson.com.br/ or https://ensino.pearson.com.br/suporte and download Multi-Rom to access audio content and others

Hello

1 Listen and chant.

Aa Bb Cc Dd Ee Ff Gg Hh Ii
Jj Kk Ll Mm Nn Oo Pp Qq Rr
Ss Tt Uu Vv Ww Xx Yy Zz

2 Listen and read.

Hello! A pink balloon, please.

Hello! What's your name?

I'm Minnie and this is Mickey.

Minnie, that's M – I – N – N – I – E. And Mickey, that's M – I – C – K – Y, right?

No, it's M – I – C – K – E – Y.

3 Now ask and answer.

What's your name?

I'm Andy. That's A – N – D – Y.

Hello: The alphabet. *I'm (Andy).*

4 **Listen and write in your notebook.**

1
Age: ?
Favorite color: ?
Lucky number: ?

2
Age: ?
Favorite color: ?
Lucky number: ?

5 **Ask and answer.**

How old are you?
I'm nine.

What's your lucky number?
Seven.

What's your favorite color?
Blue.

6 **Play with a friend.**

I can see something starting with P.
Pencil?

Hello: What's your favorite color/lucky number? *How old are you? I'm (eight).*
Numbers 1–20.

3

UNIT 1
I'm happy

1 Listen and find. CD 1.10

2 Read, listen and repeat. Then look and say *Yes* or *No*. CD 1.11

happy sad scared tired worried angry

I'm not worried. I'm happy!

3 Listen and say. CD 1.12

Vocabulary I: angry, *happy*, *sad*, scared, tired, worried. *I'm (happy). I'm not (sad).*

4

4 Look, read and say the number.

1  2  3

I'm thirsty.

4  5  6

Photo number 2.

A I'm thirsty. **B** I'm happy. **C** I'm not angry. I'm scared.

D I'm sad. **E** I'm not worried. I'm tired. **F** I'm not tired. I'm hungry.

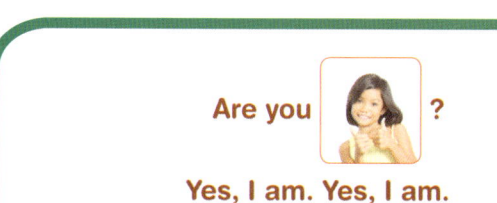

5 Read and say. Then listen and check.

Are you ___ ?
Yes, I am. Yes, I am.
I'm ___ . I'm not ___ .

Are you ___ ? 
Yes, I am. Yes, I am.
I'm ___ and ___ .

Are you ___ ?
Yes, I am. Yes, I am.
I'm very ___ .

Are you ___ ? 
No, I'm not. No, I'm not.
I'm ___ and ___ . 
Look! A monster in my bed!

Practice I: hungry, thirsty. Are you (thirsty)? *Feelings. I'm / I'm not (happy).*

6 Which person is Adam? Listen and find. [CD 1.14]

7 Look at Activity 6. Read and match.

- **A** He's hungry.
- **B** She's tired.
- **C** She's scared.
- **D** He's happy.
- **E** He's sad.
- **F** She's thirsty.

Vocabulary II: He / She's (*happy*). Feelings. I'm / I'm not (*happy*).

8 Listen and say *Yes* or *No*.

1 Is she worried?

2 Is she scared?

3 Is he sad?

4 Is he worried?

9 Tongue Twister! Listen and repeat.

S**a**m's c**a**t is h**a**ppy.
P**a**m's c**a**t is s**a**d.
D**a**n's c**a**t is **a**ngry.
Anne's c**a**t is b**a**d.

Practice II: Phonics: /æ/. Is he / she (happy)? Feelings. I'm / I'm not (happy). He / She's (happy).

10 Listen and answer.

1 Mickey and Minnie are in the forest. Minnie's scared.

Mickey! It's dark. I'm scared!

It's OK. I'm not scared.

2 Listen! Is it a ghost? I'm scared of ghosts.

3 It's OK. It isn't a ghost. It's an owl. Look!

4 Listen! What's that? Is it a monster?

5 Yes, look! It's a monster! I'm scared of monsters!

Oh, no! Now I'm scared, too!

6 Oh, Pluto! It's you!

Phew! That's OK.

Mickey isn't scared of Pluto!

11 Now act the story out.

Story: owl. I'm scared of (ghosts). *Feelings. I'm / I'm not (happy).*

UNIT 1

12 Look, read and write the number. Then answer.

1 Hi. I'm Mia. Look! I'm in the garden with my friends. I'm happy!

2 This is my friend Sam. He likes ice cream. He's hungry!

3 This is Anna. She's scared of dogs.

4 This is Tim. He's tired.

5 And this is Polly. She likes water. She's thirsty.

A Who's scared?
B Who's thirsty?
C Who's tired?
D Who's happy?
E Who's hungry?

13 Go to page 73. Cut out. Then listen and play.

Are you scared?

Yes, I'm scared!

Skills: Feelings. I'm / I'm not / He's / She's (happy). I'm scared of (dogs).

9

14 Look, read and say.

1. I'm excited.
2. I'm bored.
3. I'm surprised.

A   B   C

I'm excited. Picture B.

15 Look, read and check (✓) or cross (✗).

Look at these photos. How do you feel?
Is it a good (✓) or a bad (✗) feeling?

1. It's your birthday. You have a present.
2. You can't play with your friends.
3. You're at the amusement park.
4. Your brother has your favorite toy.

16 Project: Make a feelings poster.

Ready for life: Thinking about good and bad feelings.

REVIEW 1

1 **Listen and answer.** CD 1.19

1 – No, he isn't bored.

| happy | sad | scared | bored | tired | worried |

2 **Do the survey. Then write in your notebook.**

	happy	angry	sad	worried	hungry	thirsty
_____						
_____						
_____						
Me						

Today, _____ is _____.
Today, _____ is _____.
Today, _____ is _____.
Today, I'm _____.

Review 1: *Feelings. I'm / I'm not / He's / She's (happy). Is he / she happy? Are you happy? I'm scared of (monsters).*

11

UNIT 2 It's snowing

1 Listen and find. CD 1.20

2 Read, listen and repeat. Then look and say *Yes* or *No*. CD 1.21

hot   cold   sunny   cloudy   snowing   raining

It's cold. It's snowing.

3 Listen and say. CD 1.22

Vocabulary I: cloudy, cold, hot, raining, snowing, sunny. It's (raining).

4 Look, read and write the number. Then read and say.

It's hot and sunny. Picture number 6.

A	It's hot and sunny.	
C	It's snowing. It's cold.	
E	It's stormy.	

B	It's cloudy.	
D	It's windy.	
F	It's raining.	

5 Read and say. Then listen and check.

It's _____, it's _____, it's cold!

Here's your _____!

It's _____, it's _____, it's hot!

It's _____, it's _____, it's wet!

Here's your _____!

Here's your _____!

Practice I: stormy, windy. *Clothes. Weather. It's / It isn't (cold). What's the weather like?*

6 Listen, read and say the number. CD 1.24

1. It's spring.
2. It's summer.
3. It's fall.
4. It's winter.

7 Listen, find and say. Then write in your notebook. CD 1.25

I like …

1. Sarah
2. Ben
3. James
4. Molly

Vocabulary II: fall, spring, summer, winter. *Weather. It's / It isn't (snowing).*

14

8 Listen, read and say 1 or 2.

1 It isn't cloudy. It's hot and sunny.

2 It isn't hot. It's snowing.

9 Tongue Twister! Listen and repeat.

There's a **mou**se on a cl**ou**d.
There's a sn**ow**man in a b**oa**t.

Practice II: Phonics: /aʊ/ vs. /əʊ/. What's the weather like? Seasons. Weather. It's / It isn't (snowing).

15

10 Listen and answer.

1. Goofy's in the garden. It's hot and sunny.
Ah, it's hot!

2. Oh! It's windy now!

3. Oh! My hat!

4. Oh, no! It's stormy now! I don't like stormy weather.

5. Ah! There's my hat!

6. Goofy! You're wet!
Yes, but I have my hat!

11 Now act the story out.

Story: wet. *Clothes. Seasons. Weather. It's / It isn't (snowing).*

UNIT 2

12 **Read and say *Yes* or *No*. In your notebook, correct the sentences that are wrong.**

1. It's summer. It's hot and sunny.

2. It's windy. It isn't spring. It's fall.

3. It's winter. It's snowing. She's wearing a hat and a scarf.

4. It isn't sunny. It's raining. He's wearing a raincoat.

13 **Go to page 75. Cut out. Then listen and play.**

Snap! It's raining!

Skills: *Clothes. Seasons. Weather. It's / It isn't (snowing). What's the weather like?*

17

14 Read, listen and write the missing months. CD 1.30

**Look at the calendar.
There are 12 months in a year.**

January _____ _____ April

May _____ July _____

September _____ November _____

15 Read and guess the month. Then say the number.

What's the month?

It's hot and sunny. I'm not at school. I'm on vacation. It's …

I'm excited. It's Christmas and I have lots of presents. It's …

It's spring. It's Children's Day. I don't go to school.

It's sunny. I have some chocolate eggs. It's …

1 2 3 4

16 Project: Make a calendar.

Ready for life: Thinking about the changing seasons and weather.

18

REVIEW 2

1 Read and say the missing words.

> raining   coat   winter   hot

1 It's ❓.
2 It isn't ❓.
3 It isn't ❓.
4 She's wearing a ❓.

2 In your notebook, draw and write about the weather today. Then tell a friend.

Today, it's windy.
It isn't sunny.

Review 2: *Clothes. Seasons. Weather. It's / It isn't (snowing). What's the weather like?*

UNIT 3
I'm dancing

1 Listen and find. CD 1.31

2 Read, listen and repeat. Then look and say *Yes* or *No*. CD 1.32

dancing   jumping   running   singing   talking   walking

I'm jumping!

3 Listen and say. CD 1.33

Vocabulary I: dancing, jumping, running, singing, talking, walking. I'm (dancing).

4 Listen, read and say the number. Then play.

1. He's dancing.
2. She's singing.
3. He's swimming.
4. She's drawing.
5. He's reading.
6. She's writing.

5 Read and say. Then listen and check.

Look, I'm [dancing], and I'm [singing], too.

Look, I'm [drawing], and I'm [running], too.

Now I'm [reading], and I'm [writing], too.

Now I'm [walking], and I'm [whispering] to you.

Practice 1: drawing, reading, swimming, writing. He / She's (drawing). *Actions. I'm (dancing).*

21

6 **Listen, find and repeat.** CD 1.36

7 **Listen and say. Then write in your notebook.** CD 1.37

1 I'm dancing.
2 I'm juggling.
3 I'm jumping.
4 I'm singing.
5 I'm talking.
6 I'm walking.

couch

spoon

plate

cup

bowl

8 **Read and say *Yes* or *No*.**

1 The closet is talking.
2 The plate is jumping.
3 The cup is singing.
4 The chair is dancing.
5 The couch is juggling.
6 The bowl is walking.

Vocabulary II: bowl, closet, couch, cup, plate, spoon; closet; juggling.
Actions. I'm / He's / She's (dancing).

closet

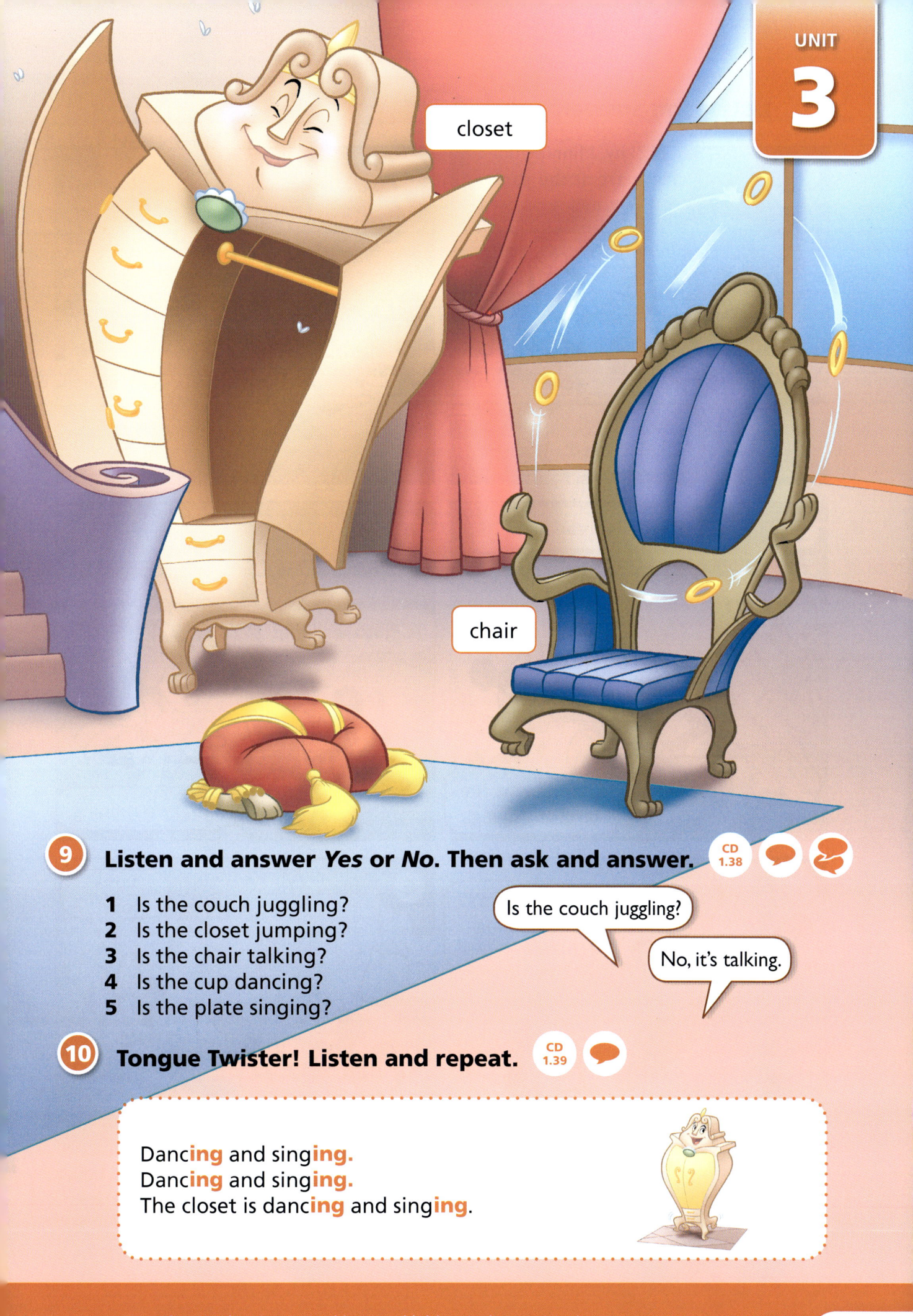

chair

UNIT **3**

9 **Listen and answer *Yes* or *No*. Then ask and answer.**

1. Is the couch juggling?
2. Is the closet jumping?
3. Is the chair talking?
4. Is the cup dancing?
5. Is the plate singing?

Is the couch juggling?

No, it's talking.

10 **Tongue Twister! Listen and repeat.**

Danc**ing** and sing**ing**.
Danc**ing** and sing**ing**.
The closet is danc**ing** and sing**ing**.

Practice II: Phonics: /ŋ/. Is (the couch) (dancing)? Yes, it's dancing. *Actions. Furniture. I'm / He's / She's (dancing).*

11 Listen and answer.

1. Mickey, Minnie and Pluto are at the park.
Go, Pluto! Oh, I'm tired!

2. Pluto isn't tired. Look! He's swimming.

3. Pluto, I'm reading.
Oh! Look at the bird! It's flying!

4. Is Pluto walking?
No, he's running.

5. Now he's jumping. Pluto, stop!

6. Look out!
Oh, no! Mickey isn't happy.

12 Now act the story out.

Story: *Actions. I'm / He's / She's / It's (dancing). Is Pluto (walking)?*

UNIT 3

13 Read and find. Then write in your notebook.

I'm **Max**. Can you see me? I'm running. Look at my sister, **Maria**. Is she running? No, she's swimming. My brother, **Simon**, is dancing. Look at my **dad**. Is he reading? Yes, he's reading, and my **mom'**s walking.

Max. Number 1.

14 Go to page 77. Cut out. Then listen and play.

She's singing. It's flying.

She's singing. She's singing. They're the same.

Skills: *Actions. I'm / He's / She's / It's (dancing).*

25

15 Read, listen and write the number. CD 1.42

Olympic Champions!

Olympic gold medal

Tomasz Majewski is throwing the ball. He's very strong. He can throw 21 meters! He has two Olympic gold medals.

1

2
This is **Usain Bolt**. He's running. He can run very fast. He's the world champion and he has six Olympic gold medals!

3
Jessica Ennis is jumping. She can run very fast, too. And she can throw. She has one Olympic gold medal.

4
This is **Missy Franklin**. She's swimming. She can swim very fast. She has four Olympic gold medals.

A He's running fast. ☐   B He's throwing the ball. ☐

C She's swimming. ☐   D She's jumping. ☐

16 Project: Make a poster about some Olympic champions or sports.

Ready for life: *Thinking about the importance of working hard.*

REVIEW 3

1 **Listen and answer *Yes* or *No*. Then read and say.**
CD 1.43

1 It's flying.
3 It's singing.
5 He's reading a book.

2 It's dancing.
4 It's flying.
6 She's talking to the bird.

2 **In your notebook, write five sentences about what your family and friends are doing. Then tell a friend.**

My mom is dancing.
My dad isn't reading. He's talking to my brother.
My sister is singing.
Our pet bird is flying.
I'm writing.

Review 3: *Actions. I'm / He's / She's / It's (dancing).*

UNIT 4
There's a park

1 Listen and find. (CD 1.44)

2 Read, listen and repeat. Then look and say *Yes* or *No*. (CD 1.45)

store café school library park garage

There's a garage. There isn't a school.

3 Listen and say. (CD 1.46)

Vocabulary I: café, garage, library, park, school, store. There isn't a (school). *There's a (store).*

4 Read, listen and repeat. Then say. CD 1.47

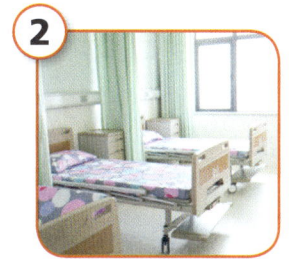

1. movie theater
2. hospital
3. hotel
4. museum

5 Listen and say *Yes* or *No*. Then read and say. CD 1.48

1. There is / There isn't a hospital.
2. There are five stores.

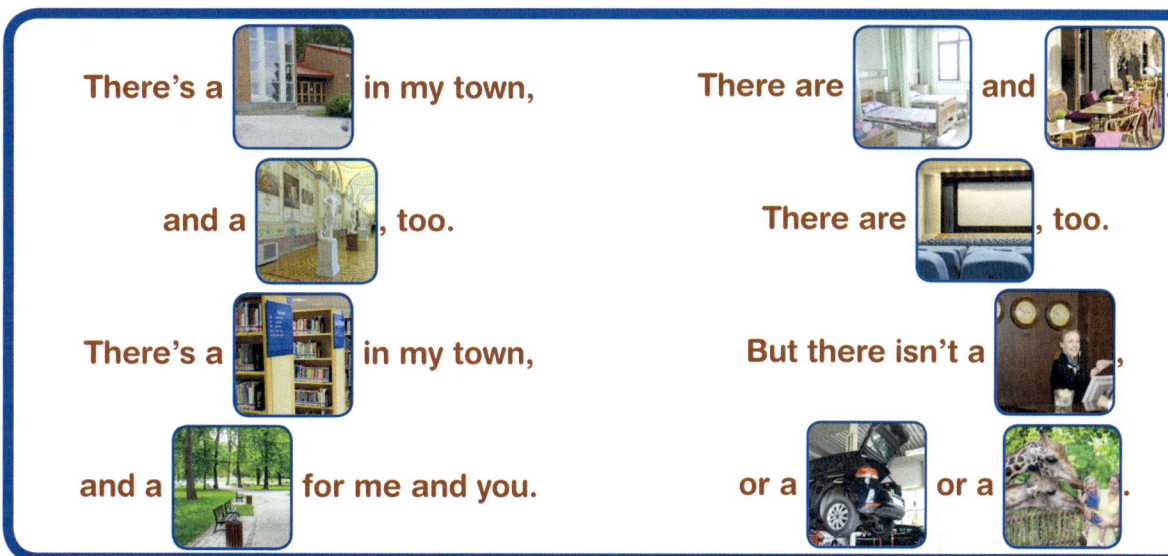

6 Read and say. Then listen and check. CD 1.49

There's a ____ in my town, and a ____, too.

There's a ____ in my town, and a ____ for me and you.

There are ____ and ____.
There are ____, too.
But there isn't a ____, or a ____ or a ____.

Practice I: hospital, hotel, movie theater, museum. There are (two stores). *Places in town. There is / isn't a (park).*

29

7 Where's the cat? Listen, find and circle. CD 1.50

1 in front of

2 next to

3 behind

8 Listen and say the number. CD 1.51

9 Look at Activity 8. Ask and answer.

Where's the school?

It's next to the hospital.

Vocabulary II: behind, in front of, *next to*. Where's the (school)? *Places in town*.

30

UNIT 4

y 1 or 2. Then read and write the

eum.   ☐   B   There are cars in front of a café. ☐
rown car. ☐   D   There are two red cars. ☐
afé. ☐   F   There is a green car. ☐

er! Listen and repeat. 🎧 CD 1.53 💬

There's a sh**a**rk in a c**a**r in the p**a**rk.
He's j**u**mping, r**u**nning and j**u**ggling.

ce II: Phonics: /ɑː/ vs /ʌ/. Places in town. Prepositions of place.
There is / isn't a (park). There are (two stores).

31

12 Listen and answer.

1. Look! There's a museum. Let's go in!
   But Mickey, I'm tired!

2. Oh, look! ...are old

3. Oh, look! There's a fantastic plate!
   Where's the café?

4. Look! Ther...

5. Oh, no! The plate's falling!

6. It's OK!

13 Now act the story out.

Story: falling. Feelings. Furniture. Places in town. There is / There are (four cups). Where's the (café)?

UNIT 4

14 Listen, find and say. Then write.

library   box   tree   café   hotel

1 There's a girl in front of the _____.

2 There's a boy in front of the _____.

3 There's a cat next to the _____.

4 There's a man in front of the _____.

5 There's a dog behind the _____.

15 Go to page 79. Cut out. Then listen and play.

There's a store, a museum and a café.

Where's the store?

It's next to the café.

Skills: Places in town. Prepositions of place. There is / isn't a (park). There are (two stores).

33

16 Listen and read. 🎧 CD 1.57

NEW YORK
Come to New York!

1 Central Park
There are beautiful parks. This is Central Park. You can walk in the park. There's a museum next to the park.

2 Empire State Building
The Empire State Building is very tall. You can see lots of things from it.

3 Hudson River / The Statue of Liberty
Look at the Hudson River. There are lots of boats on the river. Can you see the Statue of Liberty? It's very old.

Brooklyn Bridge
There are lots of bridges in New York. This is Brooklyn Bridge. It's old. It's very long.

4 Fifth Avenue
There are good stores on Fifth Avenue. And there are lots of yellow taxis, too!

5

• NEW YORK • NEW YORK • NEW YORK •

17 Read and write the number. What is it? 💬

A There are lots of boats on it. ☐   B It's next to a museum. ☐
C There are good stores here. ☐   D It isn't short. It's tall. ☐

18 Project: Make a poster about a city. ✏️✂️

Ready for life: *Thinking about large cities and what makes them beautiful (or not).*

REVIEW 4

1 Listen and answer. Then read and say the missing words. CD 1.58

---

seven   are   's   isn't   behind   isn't

---

1 There **?** a store.
2 The black car is **?** the red car.
3 There are **?** cars.
4 There **?** a yellow car.
5 There **?** a black car.
6 There **?** two red cars.

2 In your notebook, draw a map of your town. Write about it. Then tell a friend.

> There's a movie theater.
> There are lots of cars.
> There isn't a museum.

Review 4: Places in town. Prepositions of place. There is / isn't a (park). There are (lots of).

35

UNIT 5
My day

1 Listen and find. CD 2.1

2 Read, listen and repeat. Then look and say *Yes* or *No*. CD 2.2

get up — take a shower — have breakfast — go to school — study — have lunch

I get up, I have breakfast, I read, and then I have lunch.

3 Listen and say. CD 2.3

Vocabulary I: get up, go to school, have breakfast, have lunch, take a shower, study. I (get up).

36

4 Look and say. Then complete.

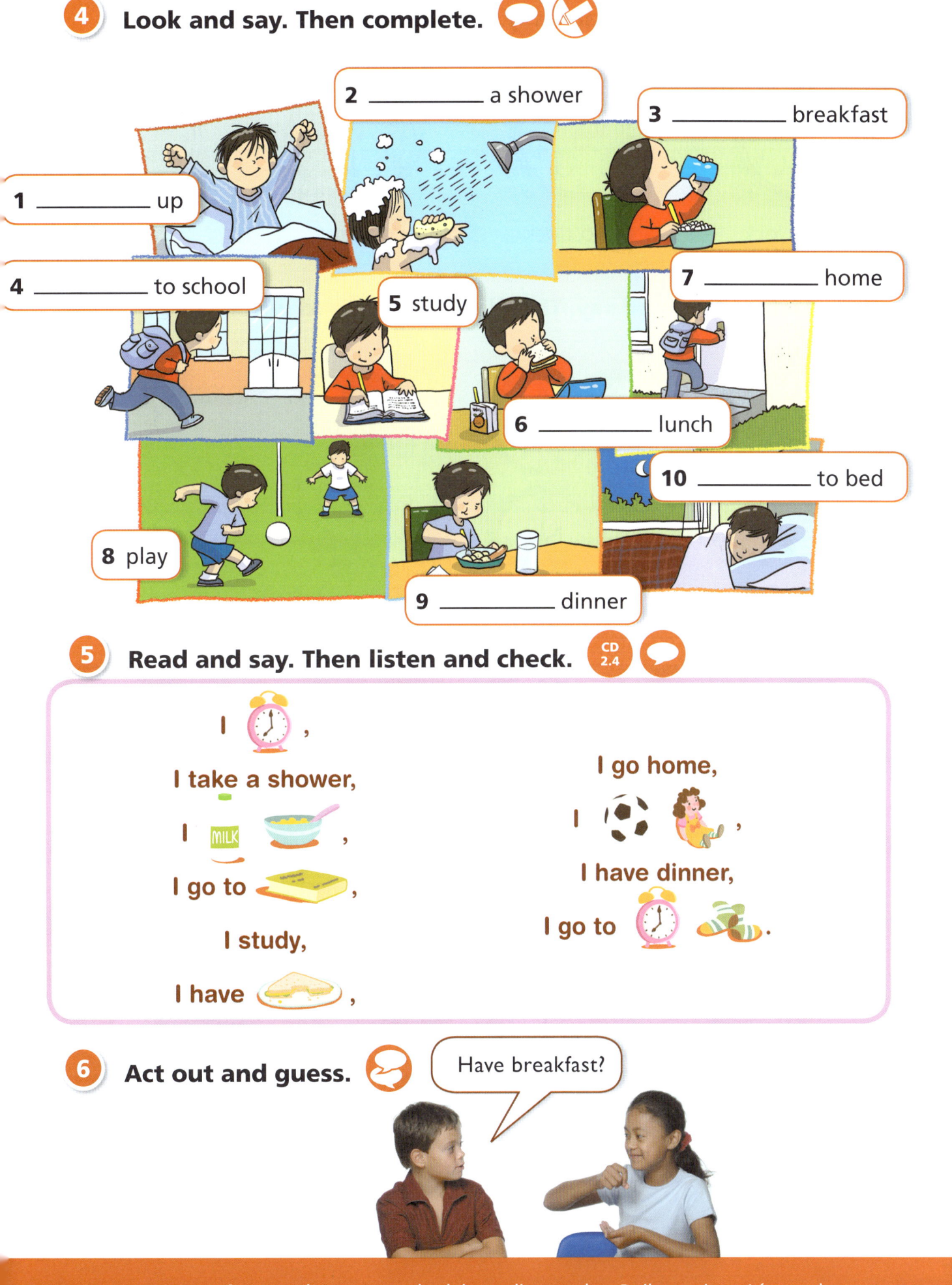

1. _____ up
2. _____ a shower
3. _____ breakfast
4. _____ to school
5. study
6. _____ lunch
7. _____ home
8. play
9. _____ dinner
10. _____ to bed

5 Read and say. Then listen and check.

I 🕰,
I take a shower,
I 🥛🥣,
I go to 📚,
I study,
I have 🥪,

I go home,
I ⚽ 🧒,
I have dinner,
I go to 🕰 🧦.

6 Act out and guess.

"Have breakfast?"

Practice I: go home, go to bed, have dinner, play. *Daily routines. I (get up).*

37

7 Listen. Then look and say.

1. one o'clock
2. ten o'clock
3. one thirty
4. five thirty

8 Listen, find and say. Then listen again and write.

1. I get up at _____ o'clock.
2. I take a shower at _____ thirty.
3. I study at _____ o'clock.
4. I have lunch at _____ thirty.
5. I play at _____ o'clock.
6. I go to bed at _____ thirty.

Vocabulary II: It's (one) o'clock. It's five thirty. *Daily routines.* I (get up) at (nine o'clock).

UNIT 5

9 Listen and match. Then read and say.

1. She gets up.
2. She plays.

a b c d e f

3. She has dinner.
4. She goes to bed.

10 Tongue Twister! Listen and repeat.

It's **cool** to go to sch**ool**.
L**oo**k. I like b**oo**ks!

Practice II: Phonics: /ʊ/ vs /uː/. Daily routines. Telling the time. I (get up) at (six o'clock).

11 Listen and answer.

1
- Mickey! Get up!
- Oh, no! I'm tired!

2
Goofy gets up and takes a hot shower.

3 Goofy has breakfast.
- Mmm. Eggs for breakfast.
- Ugh, I'm not hungry.

4
- Come on! We're late.
- Goofy, it's dark! What time is it?

5
- It's nine o'clock! Look!

6
- Uh-oh!
- No, Goofy. It's two thirty. It's early!

Mickey and Goofy go back to bed!

12 Now act the story out.

Story: It's early. We're late. *Daily routines. Telling the time. I (get up) at (six o'clock).*

40

UNIT 5

13 Read and say *Yes* or *No*. Then talk about your day.

1. I'm Alex. I get up at eight o'clock.
2. I go to school at eight thirty.
3. I have lunch at twelve thirty.
4. I go home at three thirty.
5. I have dinner at six thirty.
6. At nine o'clock I read a book and go to bed.

14 Go to page 81. Cut out. Then listen and play. CD 2.10

I go to school...

... at eight o'clock.

Skills: Daily routines. Telling the time. I (get up) at (six thirty).

41

15 Listen and read. CD 2.11

This is our Earth.

It goes round and round.

Every day, half of the Earth is in the sun.
For people here it's daytime.

But half of the Earth is dark.
For people here it's night.

It's daytime.

It's night.

Tomek lives in Poland.
Kimi lives in Japan.
When it's daytime in Poland, it's night in Japan.

16 Read and say *Yes* or *No*. Then correct the sentences in your notebook.

1. The Earth goes up and round.
2. Every day, half of the Earth is dark.
3. When it's daytime in Poland, it's daytime in Japan.
4. When Kimi has breakfast, Tomek has dinner.

17 Project: Make a poster about your daily routine.

Ready for life: *Learning that it can be day or night at the same time for people living in different parts of our planet.*

REVIEW 5

1 Listen and write the times. Then say the times. CD 2.12

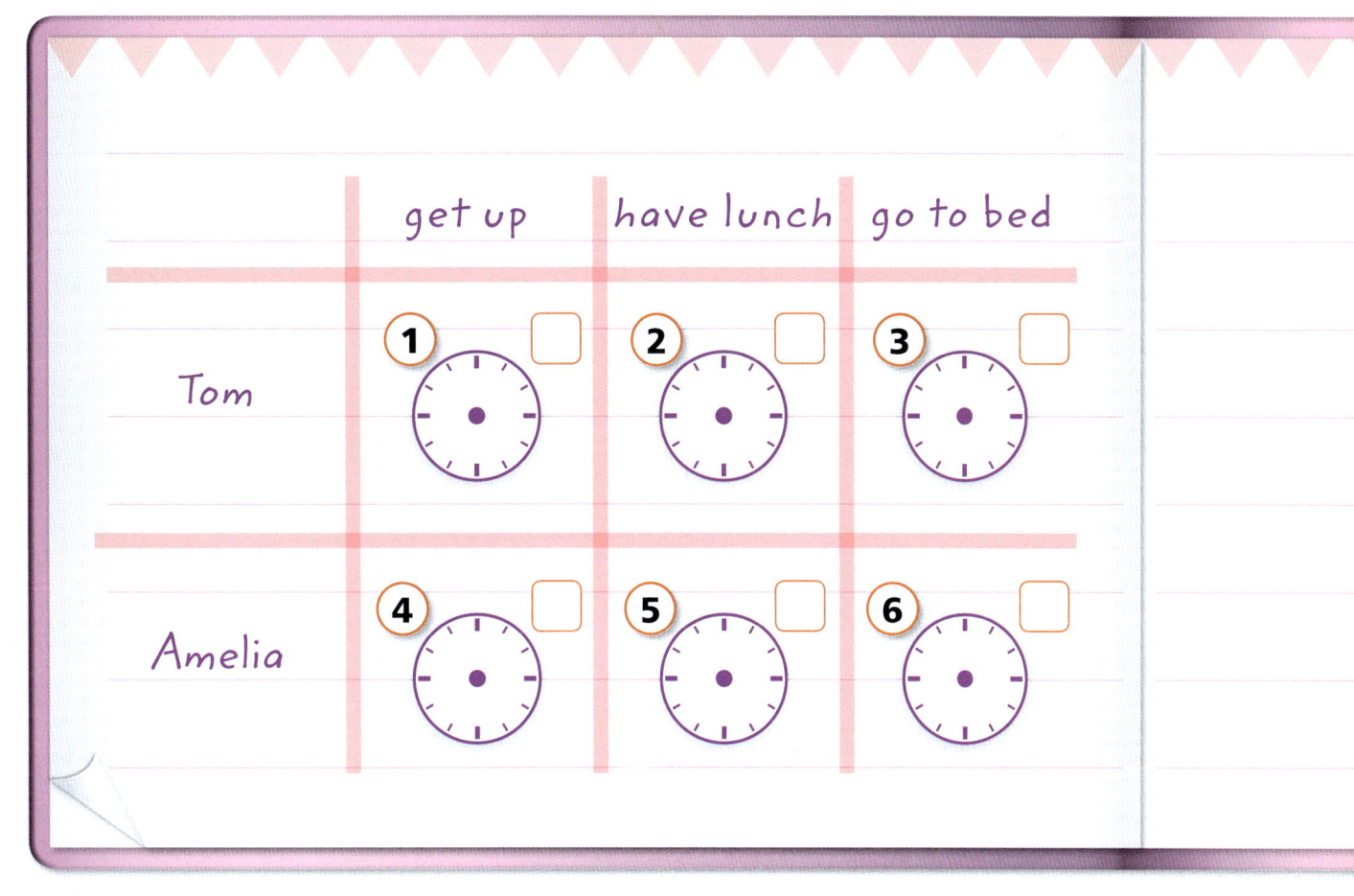

	get up	have lunch	go to bed
Tom	1	2	3
Amelia	4	5	6

2 In your notebook, write about your dream day. Then tell a friend.

On my dream day, I get up at eleven o'clock. I have breakfast. I don't go to school. I go to the park with my friends. I have lunch at one thirty. I eat pizza.

Review 5: *Daily routines. Telling the time. I (get up) at (six thirty).*

UNIT 6 — My hobbies

1 Listen and find. CD 2.13

2 Read, listen and repeat. Then look and say *Yes* or *No*. CD 2.14

go camping   go cycling   go fishing   go hiking   go running   go swimming

I go hiking and camping.

3 Listen and say. CD 2.15

Vocabulary I: go camping / cycling / fishing / hiking / *running* / *swimming*.
I go *(swimming)*.

4 Look, read and write the number. Then say.

1 **2** **3**

4 **5** **6**

A I do karate.
B I have art lessons.
C I have music lessons.
D I do gymnastics.
E I do ballet.
F I have English lessons.

I do karate. Photo number 6.

5 Read and say. Then listen and check. CD 2.16

I go 👓 ,
I go cycling,
I go 🎣 .
On the weekend, on the weekend.

I do 🩰
And gymnastics,
I do 🥋
On the weekend, on the weekend.

I have 🎨 lessons.
And 🎸 lessons.
I have fun
On the weekend, on the weekend.

Practice II: do ballet / karate; have art / English / music lessons. I (have art lessons) on weekends. *Hobbies. I go (swimming).*

45

6 Listen, find and say.

**MONDAY   TUESDAY
WEDNESDAY   THURSDAY   FRIDAY
SATURDAY   SUNDAY**

7 Look, read and match. Then listen and say.

| Monday | Tuesday | Wednesday | Thursday |
| Friday | Saturday | Sunday | |

1 She has an art lesson   A on Friday.
2 She goes swimming   B on Thursday.
3 She has a music lesson   C on Sunday.
4 She does ballet   D on Monday.
5 She does karate   E on Saturday.
6 She goes camping   F on Tuesday.
7 She goes cycling   G on Wednesday.

> She has an art lesson on Monday.

Vocabulary II: Days of the week. She (goes swimming) on (Monday). *Hobbies.*

UNIT 6

8 **Copy the table in your notebook. Then listen and complete with the missing information.** CD 2.19

What does Russell do on...	
Monday	?
Tuesday	?
Wednesday	?
Thursday	?
Friday	?
Saturday Sunday	?

9 **Tongue Twister! Listen and repeat.** CD 2.20

Six hippos go fishing and swimming.

I like cheese and green trees.

Practice II: *He has / does / goes (art lessons / karate / swimming) on (Monday).*
Phonics: /iː/ vs /ɪ/. Days of the week. Hobbies. I (go) (swimming).

47

10 Listen and answer.

1.
— Is it Friday today?
— It's… um… Yes, it's Friday.

2.
— What do you do on Friday?
— I do karate!

3.

4.
— It's Thursday today. We do ballet on Thursday.
— Oh, no!

5.
— Help! I don't do ballet. I do karate!

6.
— Goofy, it isn't Friday. It's Thursday!
— Sorry, Mickey!

11 Now act the story out.

Story: *Days of the week. Hobbies.* I (do) / don't (do) (karate) on (Friday).

48

UNIT 6

12 Read and say the name. Then listen and check.

Monday
Wednesday
Friday
Saturday

Monday
Tuesday
Friday
Saturday

Sam

I go swimming on Monday.
I have a music lesson on Wednesday.
I go cycling on Friday.
I do karate on Saturday.
Who am I?

Lucy

13 Go to page 83. Cut out. Then listen and play.

She goes hiking on Friday.

She goes hiking on Saturday.

Skills: Days of the week. Hobbies. I (go) (swimming) on (Monday).
He / She (does) (ballet) on the weekend.

49

14 **Listen and read.** CD 2.24

www.scoutcamps.coox

Fun and adventure!

Scouts is about having fun and adventure and helping people. There are Boy Scouts and Girl Scouts groups for people from 5 to 17. You can do lots of exciting activities and make new friends.

You can:

go camping and hiking

go kayaking

go climbing

do archery

You can learn new things and get badges, for example:

swimming   cycling   art

You can wear a Scout uniform with a special scarf called a neckerchief.

Come and have fun. Join the Scouts today!

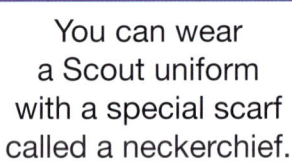

15 **Read and match.**

1 Scouts is about fun and
2 You can go
3 You can do
4 Scouts wear a sweater and

A a scarf.
B archery.
C adventure.
D kayaking.

16 **Project: Make a poster about fun and adventure.**

CLIL: *Thinking about having fun and learning new things with others.*

REVIEW 6

1 Read, listen and write *Yes* or *No*. Then say.

On the weekend…
1. he goes camping. _____
2. he goes fishing. _____
3. he has an art lesson. _____
4. he does ballet. _____
5. he goes climbing. _____
6. he goes hiking. _____

2 In your notebook, make notes about your dream week and write about it. Then tell a friend.

My Dream Week

Monday: go swimming
Tuesday: have an art lesson
Wednesday: do karate
Thursday: go fishing
Friday: have a music lesson
Saturday: play all day!

In my dream week, I go swimming on Monday.

Review 6: Days of the week. Hobbies. I (go) (swimming) on (Monday). He / She (does) (ballet) on the weekend.

UNIT 7 Lions eat meat

1 Listen and find. (CD 2.26)

2 Read, listen and repeat. Then look and say *Yes* or *No*. (CD 2.27)

antelope   crocodile   fruit   grass    leaves    meat

3 Listen and say. (CD 2.28)

Crocodiles eat meat ... and birds!

Vocabulary I: antelope, crocodile; fruit, grass, leaves, meat. *Animals.* (Crocodiles) eat (meat).

4 Look and match. Then listen, check and say. CD 2.29

Lions eat meat.

1. crocodile
2. frog
3. antelope
4. bird

bugs
seeds 
grass 
meat 

5 Read and say. Then listen and check. CD 2.30

Frogs and birds eat [bugs].

Fish eat [bugs].

Zebras and giraffes eat [grass].

Hippos and rhinos eat [grass].

Crocodiles and snakes eat [meat].

Lions eat [meat].

Tigers eat meat, too. Yes, they do!

Practice I: frog; bugs, seeds. *(Frogs)* eat *(bugs)*. Animals. Animal food.

53

6 Listen, find and say *Yes* or *No*. Then write in your notebook. CD 2.31

A Frogs eat ?.
B Giraffes eat ?.
C Antelopes eat ?.
D Monkeys eat ?.
E Lions eat ?.

meat

bugs

Lions eat grass.

No. Lions don't eat grass. They eat meat.

7 Read and circle. Then play.

1 Frogs   eat / **don't eat**   bugs.
2 Antelopes   eat / **don't eat**   meat.
3 Monkeys   **eat** / don't eat   fruit.
4 Giraffes   **eat** / don't eat   fruit.
5 Lions   eat / **don't eat**   bugs.

Vocabulary II: Lions don't eat (grass). *Animals. Animal food. (Lions) eat (meat).*

54

UNIT 7

fruit

leaves

grass

8 **Listen and say the number. Then ask and answer.** CD 2.32

What do lions eat?   Lions eat meat.

9 **Tongue Twister! Listen and repeat.** CD 2.33

Do z**e**bras **ea**t m**ea**t? No, z**e**bras **ea**t l**ea**ves.

Practice II: Phonics: /e/ vs /iː/. What do (lions) eat? *Animals. Animal food. (Lions) eat / don't eat (meat).*

55

10 Listen and answer. CD 2.34

1. Oh, look, Mickey! There are some monkeys!
   I like monkeys!

2. What do monkeys eat? Do they eat bananas?

3. Yes, they eat bananas. Monkeys eat fruit.
   Oh...!

4. Oh, no! They eat sandwiches and cakes, too!

5. Mmm. Do monkeys eat ice cream?
   No! Monkeys don't eat ice cream.

6. Yes, Mickey. Monkeys eat ice cream.
   Oh, dear!
   I don't like monkeys now!

11 Now act the story out.

Story: Animals. Food. (Lions) eat / don't eat (meat). What do (lions) eat?

56

UNIT 7

12 Look, read and write the animals.

1
They have big teeth.
They can swim.
They eat meat.
They're _____.

2
They're brown.
They can run very fast.
They eat grass.
They're _____.

3
They're small.
They can climb trees.
They eat fruit and seeds.
They're _____.

4
They have long legs.
They're yellow and brown.
They eat leaves.
They're _____.

13 Go to page 85. Cut out. Then listen and play.

No, giraffes don't eat meat.

Yes, antelopes eat grass.

Skills: Animals. Animal food. (Lions) eat / don't eat (meat). What do (lions) eat?

57

14 Listen, read and say. CD 2.36

1 Some animals eat only meat. They are carnivores. Lions, tigers and crocodiles are carnivores. They have big, sharp teeth.

sharp teeth

2 Some animals eat only plants. They are herbivores. Zebras, antelopes and hippos are herbivores. They have flat teeth.

flat teeth

3 Some animals eat meat and plants. They are omnivores. They have sharp teeth and flat teeth. Monkeys, birds and frogs are omnivores. People are omnivores, too!

4 Birds don't have teeth. They have beaks to eat seeds and bugs. Some birds have sharp beaks to eat fish and meat.

beak

What about you? Are you a herbivore, a carnivore or an omnivore?

15 Read and say *Yes* or *No*.

1 Antelopes have sharp teeth.
2 Lions have flat teeth.
3 Monkeys have sharp and flat teeth.
4 Birds don't have teeth.

16 Project: Make a poster about carnivores, herbivores and omnivores.

Ready for life: *Learning about the wonders of nature: teeth are suited to what you eat.*

58

REVIEW 7

1 Read and write.

1 Lions eat _____. They don't eat _____. (**grass / meat**)

2 Antelopes eat _____. They don't eat _____. (**fruit / grass**)

3 Monkeys eat _____. They don't eat _____. (**grass / fruit**)

4 Crocodiles eat _____. They don't eat _____. (**seeds / meat**)

2 In your notebook, write about two animals that you like. Then tell a friend.

> Giraffes are orange and brown. They have long necks and legs. They eat leaves. They don't eat meat. They are herbivores.

Review 7: Animals. Animal food. (Lions) eat / don't eat (meat). What do (lions) eat?

59

UNIT 8 I like surfing

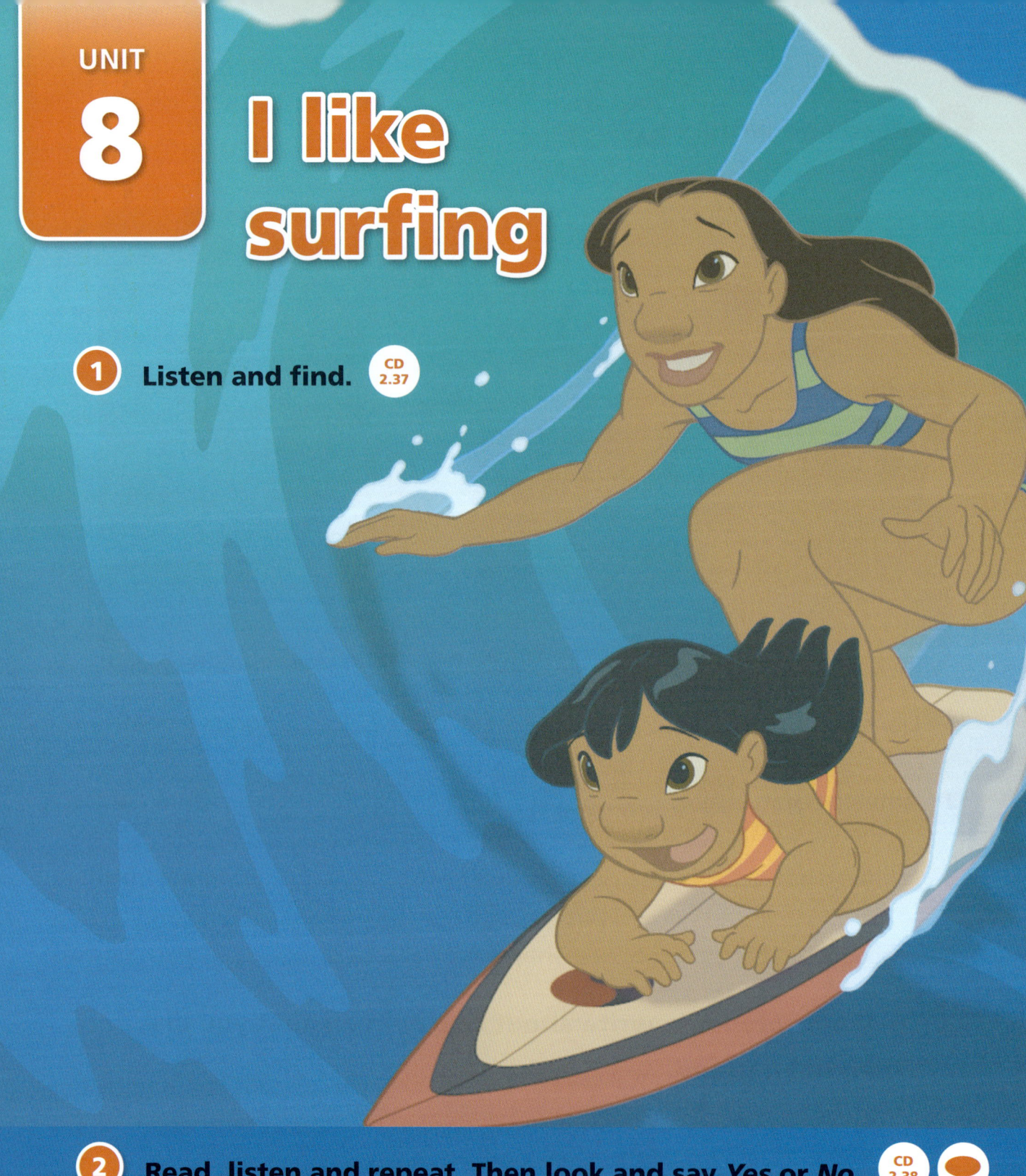

1 Listen and find. CD 2.37

2 Read, listen and repeat. Then look and say *Yes* or *No*. CD 2.38

swimming    surfing    diving    roller skating    horseback riding

I like surfing

3 Listen and say. CD 2.39

Vocabulary I: diving, horseback riding, roller skating, surfing, *swimming*. I like *(swimming)*.

60

4 Listen and say *Yes* or *No*.
Then write in your notebook. CD 2.40

1. tennis
2. ballet
3. karate
4. soccer
5. baseball
6. basketball

Photo number 1. Yes, I like tennis.

5 Read and say. Then listen and check. CD 2.41

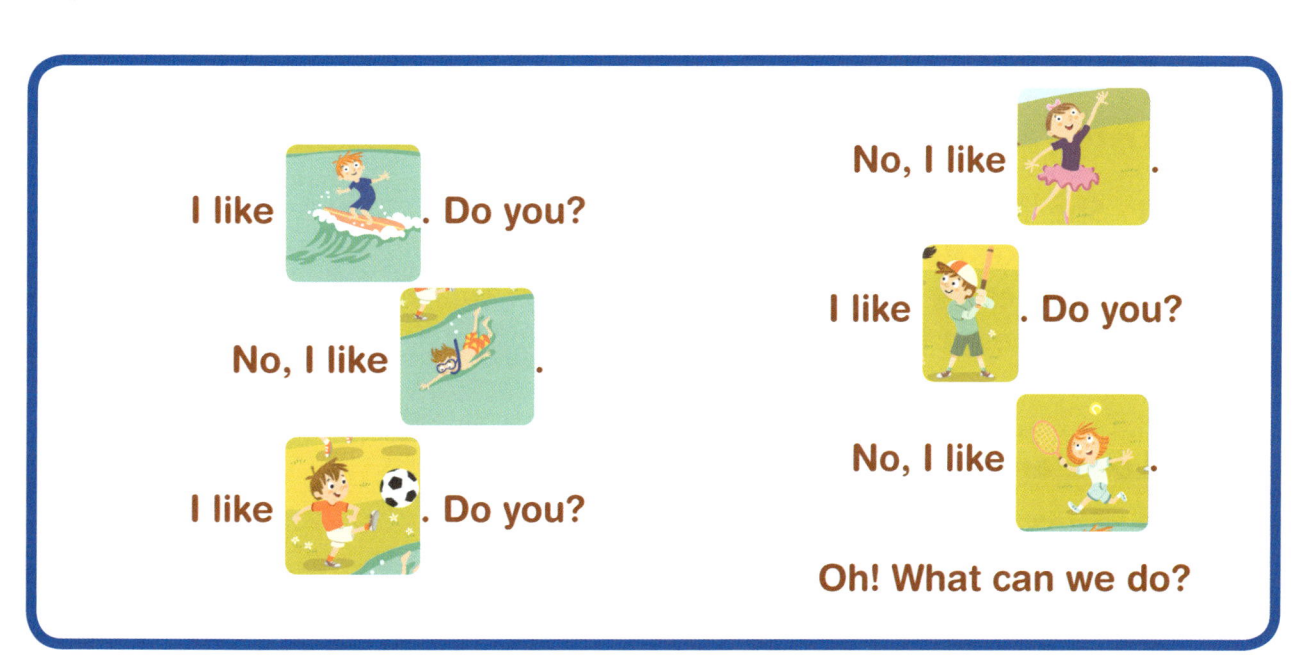

I like . Do you?

No, I like .

I like . Do you?

No, I like .

I like . Do you?

No, I like .

Oh! What can we do?

Practice I: baseball, basketball. I don't like *(diving)*. Do you like *(basketball)*? *Sports. I like (tennis).*

61

swimsuit

6 Listen and answer. Then write in your notebook. CD 2.42

1 She likes [?].
2 She likes [?].
3 He likes [?].
4 He doesn't like [?].

7 Look and write in your notebook.

1 She's wearing an orange and yellow [?].
2 He's wearing blue and red [?].
3 She has a red [?].

Vocabulary II: surfboard, swimsuit. He / She likes (*swimming*). He / She doesn't like (*diving*). *Sports.*

UNIT 8

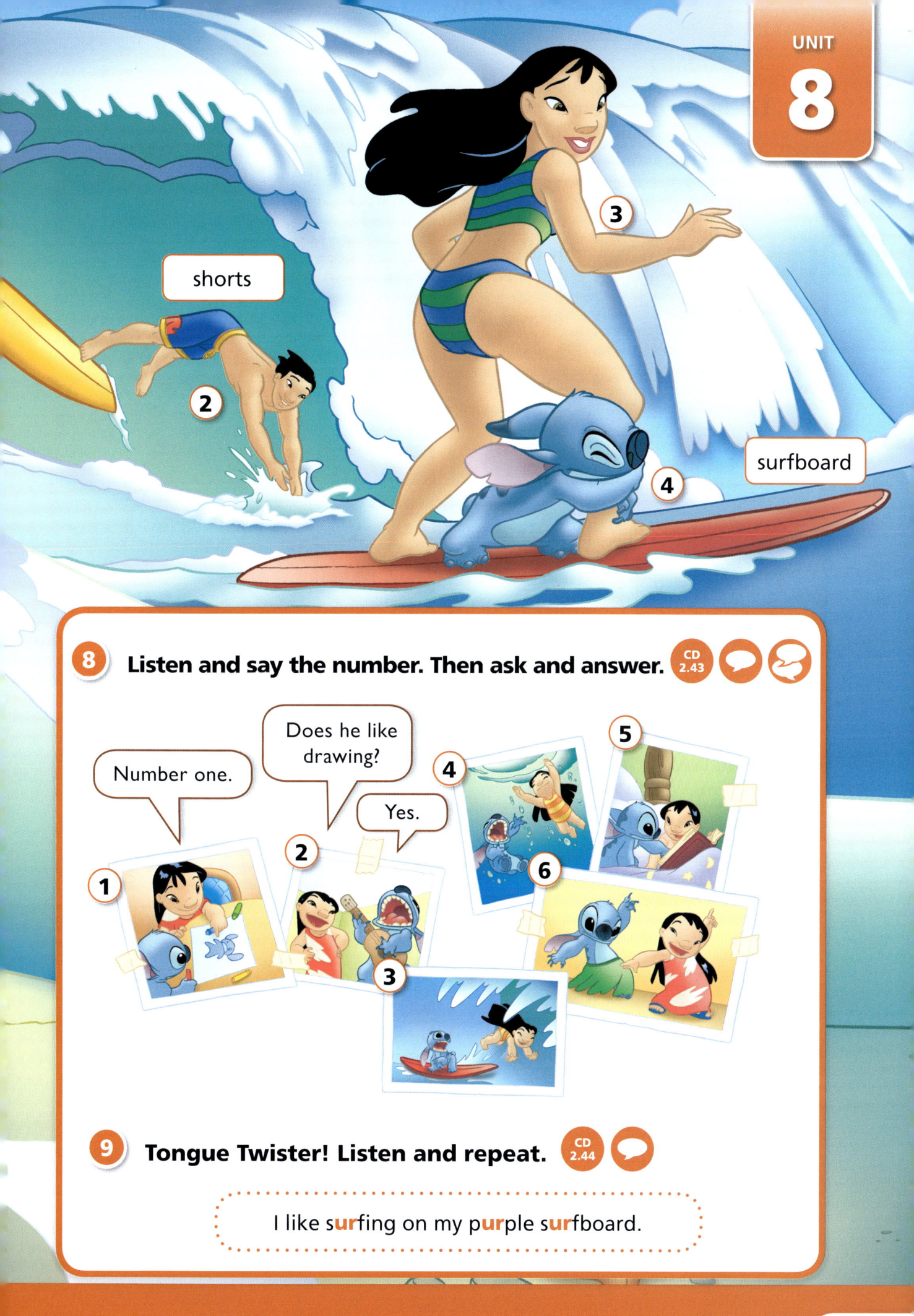

shorts

surfboard

8 Listen and say the number. Then ask and answer.

Number one.

Does he like drawing?

Yes.

9 Tongue Twister! Listen and repeat.

I like **sur**fing on my p**ur**ple s**ur**fboard.

Practice II: Phonics: /ɜː/. Does he / she like (swimming)? Sports. Yes. / No.

63

10 **Listen and answer.**

1
- Do you like tennis, Goofy?
- Oh, yes!
- Here's a racket. Let's play!

2
- I like tennis!
- Me too! This is fun.

3
- Does Pluto like tennis?
- Yes, Pluto likes tennis too.

4
- And he likes jumping!

5
- Does Minnie like tennis?
- Oh, no! No, Minnie doesn't like tennis!

6
- I'm sorry, Minnie!
- You're right, Mickey. I don't like tennis.

11 **Now act the story out.**

Story: racket. *Sports. I like / don't like (tennis). He / She likes / doesn't like (swimming). Do you like (tennis?) Does he / she like (jumping)? Yes. / No.*

64

UNIT 8

12 **Listen, find and say. Then choose and write in your notebook.** CD 2.46

1. Tom's wearing blue shorts. He likes swimming and ❓ .

2. Sam's wearing shorts and a T-shirt. He has a red racket. He likes ❓ .

3. Mia's wearing a green swimsuit. She has a yellow surfboard. She likes ❓ .

4. Anna's wearing a black hat and black boots. She has a horse. She likes ❓ .

| tennis | diving | surfing | horseback riding |

13 **Go to page 87. Cut out. Then listen and play.** CD 2.47

Do you like horseback riding?

No.

Do you like roller skating?

Yes.

Skills: *Sports. I like / don't like (tennis). He / She likes / doesn't like (swimming). Do you like (tennis?) Yes. / No.*

65

14 Listen and read. CD 2.48

www.extremsport.coox

EXTREME SPORTS

1 climbing

2 rodeo riding

3 scuba diving

Jez likes horseback riding. His favorite sport is rodeo riding. His horse runs round and round and jumps up. Jez sometimes falls off the horse.

Anton likes swimming. His favorite sport is scuba diving. He likes all the fish, and sharks, too! He isn't scared but he is very careful. Scuba diving is exciting!

Mo likes hiking and climbing. Every Saturday she goes rock climbing. She climbs very high rocks. It's her favorite sport.

15 Who likes these sports? Write the name next to the sport.

_____ swimming   _____ horseback riding   _____ climbing

16 Project: Make a poster about extreme sports.

Ready for life: *Thinking about the importance of safety when you do extreme sports.*

66

REVIEW 8

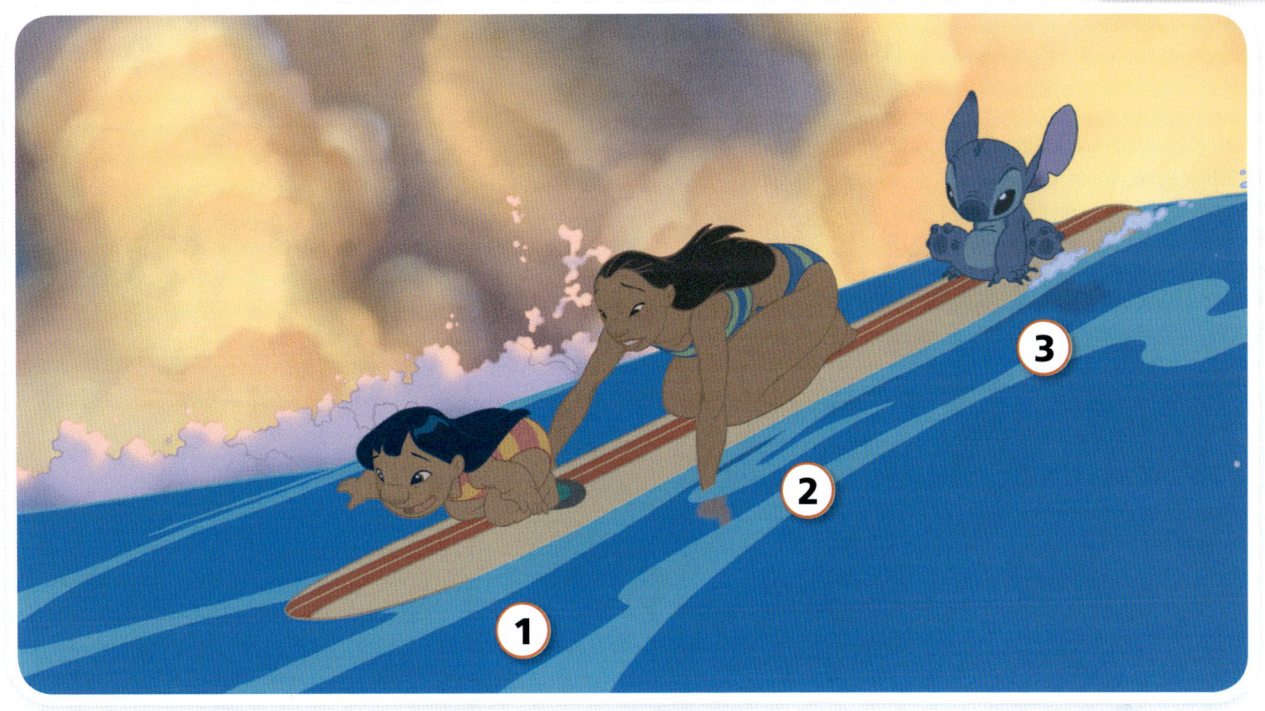

1 Look, read and circle. Then say.

1. She likes **surfing** / horseback riding.
2. She's wearing a blue and green **swimsuit** / hat.
3. He likes / **doesn't like** surfing.
4. They have a racket / **surfboard**.

2 Talk to a friend. In your notebook, write about you and your friend. Then say.

> I like roller skating.
> I don't like tennis.
> My friend is Lilian. She likes
> roller skating, too.
> She doesn't like ballet.

Review 8: Sports. I like / don't like (tennis). He / She likes / doesn't like (swimming). Do you like (tennis?) Does he / she like (jumping)?

67

Harvest Festival

1 Listen, read and find. CD 2.50

Some festivals are different in the UK and the USA. This is a British festival.

1. corn doll
2. pumpkin
3. bread
4. carrots
5. apples
6. pears
7. corn

It's fall. It's the Harvest Festival. At Harvest Festival we say 'Thank you' for our food.

2 Look at Activity 1. Count and say. Then write the numbers in your notebook.

3 Project: Design a corn doll.

Harvest Festival: *apples, bread, carrots,* corn, corn doll, *pears, pumpkin;* harvest. *Food. Seasons.*

Bonfire Night

1 **Listen, read and point.** CD 2.51

Some festivals are different in the UK and the USA. This is a British festival.

1 Guy
2 fireworks
3 bonfire
4 potatoes

Remember, remember,
The 5th of November.
Bonfires and fireworks,
Bonfires and fireworks.
Remember!

2 **Listen and say.** CD 2.52

3 **Look at Activity 1. Find and say.**

4 **Project: Make a Bonfire Night poster.**

Bonfire Night: bonfire, fireworks, guy, potatoes. *Clothes. Months.*

69

New Year's Eve

1 **Listen, read and find.** CD 2.53

1 clock
2 midnight
3 party
4 fireworks

2 **Look at Activity 1. Read, find and say.**

I'm singing.   I'm dancing.   I'm sleeping.

1   2   3

3 **Read, listen and say.** CD 2.54

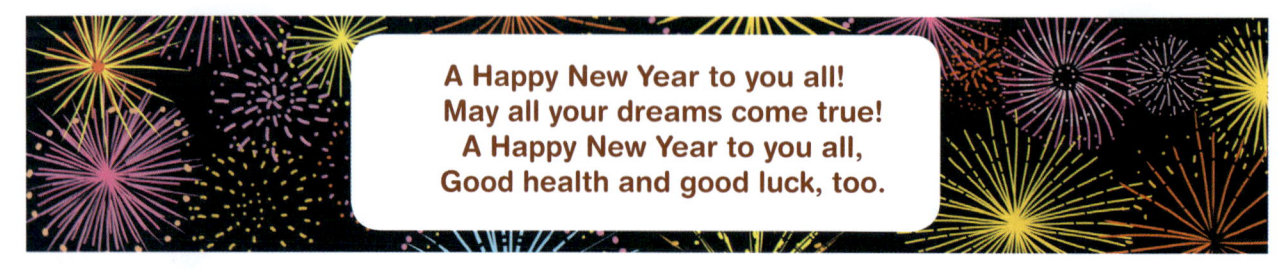

A Happy New Year to you all!
May all your dreams come true!
A Happy New Year to you all,
Good health and good luck, too.

4 **Project: New Year's Eve around the world.**

New Year's Eve: clock, *fireworks*, midnight, New Year's Eve, party.

Valentine's Day

1 Listen and say the number. CD 2.55

- **1** cake
- **2** cards
- **3** flowers
- **4** chocolates
- **5** heart

2 Find and say. Then write in your notebook.

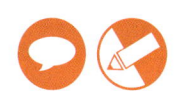

She has a ?.
He has ?.
She has a ?.
He has ?.

3 Say and play.

4 Project: Make a Valentine's Day card.

Valentine's Day: *cake*, *card*, *chocolates*, *flowers*, *heart*. I love you!

71

Mother's Day

1 Listen and say the number. CD 2.56

Happy Mother's Day, Mom!

2 Look at Activity 1 and say *Yes* or *No*.

1 Mom is behind Dad.
2 Grandma is next to Grandpa.
3 Mom has chocolates.
4 There's a cake on the table.
5 Grandma has a cup.
6 Mom's happy.

3 Project: Make some flowers for Mother's Day.

Mother's Day: *card, chocolates, flowers.* Family. Prepositions of place.

Notes

Notes

Notes

Notes

Notes

Notes

Unit 1

13 Cut out. Then listen and play.